ECOSYSTEMS

Some wild animals – such as giant pandas – get a lot of attention. But we can't protect certain animal species without looking after the entire ecosystems that they belong to. That means caring for every part of their habitat, including all the plants, minibeasts and even the teeny-tiny microbes that help keep our soils and oceans healthy and balanced.

HOW CAN WE HELP?

There's no one magic fix for protecting nature and wildlife, but there are lots of ways to help. For example, many people pressure the government to pass laws that put the planet first. Others donate or raise money to support wildlife charities, or make eco-friendly choices, such as buying fewer clothes and avoiding plastic bags.

Developing and using technologies can help us protect nature and wildlife more effectively, too. But rather than relying on hi-tech solutions to clean up our mess, it's important to protect and preserve habitats in any way we can.

DID YOU KNOW?

Over the last 50 years, we've lost around 60 per cent of Earth's vertebrate animals – that includes mammals, fish, birds and reptiles.

📷 CAMERA TRAPS

Camera traps don't actually trap wild animals – they just take their photo! These cameras are designed to blend into animals' surroundings, and to work automatically without any humans needing to be nearby, so they disturb wildlife as little as possible.

HIDDEN LIVES

A camera trap is typically left out in wild habitats for weeks, or even months. It takes photos or videos when its infrared sensor detects warm, moving objects – that is, animals (including humans) – passing in front of it.

locked weatherproof case

digital camera

infrared sensor

flash array (to help take photos at night)

Camera traps are often tied to trees along paths that animals are known to use.

Being able to 'spy' on wildlife in their natural habitat for so long helps us to learn more about animals' movements and behaviours. This helps us understand how best to help protect them – for example, by stopping roads or farms being built in areas where we know threatened species live.

Conservationists can also check up on the numbers and health of different animal populations in an area.

SECURITY CAMERAS

Some modern camera traps share photos and videos over phone and satellite networks. These networked camera traps can track humans' movements in real time, like security cameras.

This information can help local guards and police to find and question suspected intruders, show where security needs to be improved, and collect evidence to arrest and charge poachers and others who make money by harming animals and destroying their habitats.

Ocelots need protecting from poachers who want to sell them as pets or for their fur.

SHARING MEANS CARING

The photos and videos that camera traps take are a powerful part of wildlife conservation in themselves. When they are shared online, millions of people around the world can see how amazing our natural world is and be inspired to help protect it.

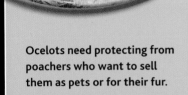

Caught on camera

☑ **First known use of a camera trap:**
George Shiras III (1859–1942), USA, 1890s – when an animal knocked into a tripwire, it triggered a camera to take a picture with a very bright, loud flash >

☑ **Average cost of a modern camera trap used for wildlife conservation:**
Around £230 to £390 >

ACOUSTIC MONITORING

Many animals use sound to 'talk' to each other, and listening in on this chatter can tell us a lot about them. Acoustic monitoring devices sense and record sound, helping us gather information about everything from individual animals' behaviour patterns to the areas in which certain species prefer to live.

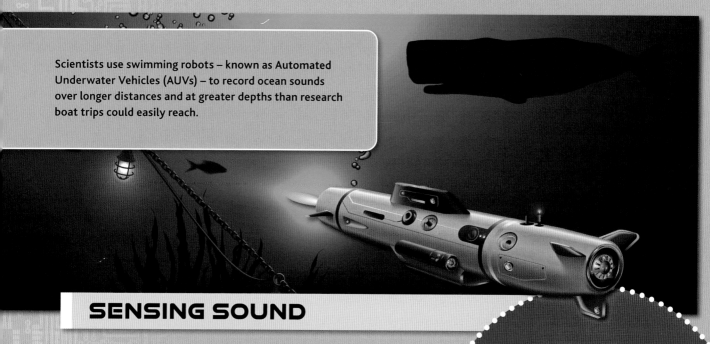

Scientists use swimming robots – known as Automated Underwater Vehicles (AUVs) – to record ocean sounds over longer distances and at greater depths than research boat trips could easily reach.

SENSING SOUND

Scientists can leave certain types of acoustic sensor out in the wild for many weeks or months, where – like camera traps (see pages 6–7) – they record nearby wild animals without disturbing them.

While camera traps mainly give us information about bigger mammals and birds, acoustic sensors can pick up sounds made by a wider range of animals, building up a helpful 'picture' of the wildlife in that area.

DID YOU KNOW?

Before recording devices existed, scientists just listened out for different birdsongs to help work out which species were living in a certain area.

BACKGROUND NOISE

Acoustic sensors pick up all sorts of sounds, not only those made by animals, and this can tell conservationists a lot about the threats facing wildlife in that area. Gunshots, chainsaws and boat engine noise could be evidence of poaching, illegal fishing and illegal logging (cutting down trees).

Scientists use this data to track patterns, such as what times of day this noise is typically heard. This can help security guards and police to be more effective at stopping illegal and harmful activity.

An acoustic recorder in use.

SOUND SOFTWARE

Acoustic monitoring can give us a huge amount of data, but this needs to be analysed in order to really be useful. Software programs can pull out important data from many hours of recording, helping scientists to track complex and long-term patterns and to better understand how species interact with each other and their environments.

In recent years, sound recording and analysing technologies have become much cheaper and more advanced. This means acoustic monitoring is now used more often as a tool to help protect nature and wildlife.

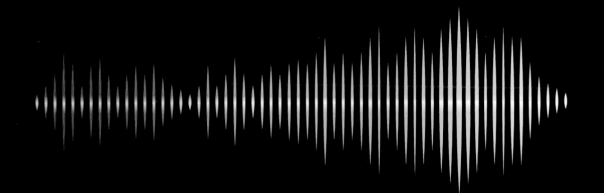

SEED BANKS

Experts believe that around one in five plant species on Earth are at risk of going extinct. Although we need to keep plants growing safely in the wild, seed banks help us to avoid a species dying out completely.

Staff wear protective clothing in the freezing Millennium Seed Bank at Wakehurst, UK.

PLANTS AT RISK

The biggest threat to a plant species' survival is their habitat being destroyed. The top three causes of this are farming, deforestation and building projects, although climate change is a growing threat.

Plants can also die from diseases. In monocultures – where lots of one crop is grown in an area – diseases can spread quickly and even wipe out entire species. It's safer to grow a wide variety of food crops, which can better survive different diseases and pests.

DID YOU KNOW?

Some plants, such as ferns, don't have seeds – they reproduce in other ways. Scientists are researching how best to protect these species from extinction.

So many species

Known plant species worldwide:
Around 390,000

Plant species used for medicine:
More than 28,000

New plant species discovered every year:
Around 2,000

POWERFUL PLANTS

It's worth protecting our planet's wide variety of plants for their own sake, and because habitats and wildlife populations often rely on particular plant species. But humans also depend on plants for food, either for eating or feeding to farm animals, and for many medicines – such as aspirin, which comes from willow tree bark and helps to reduce fever, relieve pain and prevent blood clots. We also use plants – mostly cotton – for clothes, use trees for paper, and burn wood and 'bioenergy' crops, such as corn, for fuel.

STORING SEEDS

Major seed banks, such as the Millennium Seed Bank or the Svalbard Global Seed Vault, receive seeds from all over the world. Staff examine, clean, dry (if needed), pack up and label the seeds before storing them in secure rooms at below-freezing temperatures, where they should survive for many years. When staff want to germinate these seeds – that is, grow plants from them – they place the seeds on a nutritious, jelly-like natural substance called agar and put them in a warm container called an incubator.

The Svalbard Global Seed Vault, built inside a mountain on a remote island in Norway, can store seeds from 4.5 million different crop varieties.

DNA ANALYSIS

DNA is a material that carries information about how a living thing looks and acts. It is in every cell of every living thing – including you! It has sections called genes, which carry different pieces of information.

WILD WORK

DNA

Researchers can collect, process and analyse DNA using portable kits, without having to leave the often wild, remote areas where they study nature and wildlife. This can save projects precious time and money.

DNA BARCODING

DNA barcoding involves collecting and analysing DNA samples from different plants and animals, then translating this data into a digital barcode that identifies each species. These barcodes are added to online databases, and scientists can use DNA scanners to check if the plant and animal samples they collect match any of the species on a database.

This technology sounds complicated, but it is similar to how a scanner at a supermarket checkout 'reads' the barcode printed on a packet of pasta to tell what it is and how much it costs!

Global DNA barcoding projects may help us to identify new species more quickly.

ENVIRONMENTAL DNA (eDNA)

DID YOU KNOW?

Wildlife crime officers can use handheld DNA scanners to test animal products being sold in markets or brought across countries' borders. The scanners recognise the DNA of protected animal species, which are illegal to sell.

Environmental DNA (eDNA) is found in material that plants and animals have left behind in their environment. This could be seeds, spores, pollen and sap from plants, or poo, saliva, scales and skin cells from animals.

Researchers can now collect eDNA from soil, water, snow or air samples, rather than having to find particular plants and animals to take DNA samples from them directly. This makes it quicker and less challenging to collect samples, gives us an idea of the variety of species living in an area, and avoids disturbing wildlife.

eDNA collection is particularly helpful when studying water-based habitats, because it's often very difficult to find specific plants and animals – especially in deep water.

DRONES

A drone is an aircraft that is controlled remotely, sometimes by a person many kilometres away, rather than having a pilot on board. Drones are often equipped with cameras and sensors, and can help us to protect nature and wildlife in all sorts of important ways.

Drones can be controlled from computers, tablets and smartphones.

TREE PLANTING

Drones fly over an area to gather data about the soil conditions and best locations for planting. They then drop pods – containing a seed that has started growing into a tree, plus the nutrients it needs – onto the ground.

This is a quick way to reforest large, remote areas, but the lack of control over where the pods fall could cause many trees to fail early on and die – or create forests at risk of fire because trees are too tightly packed together.

DID YOU KNOW?

Drones can plant up to two trees per second – that's 60 times faster than humans!

FIGHTING FIRES

Firefighters battling huge forest fires can send drones up high above the flames to get a bird's-eye view of where and how fast the fire is moving. This helps them plan how best to contain and put out the blaze, without risking pilots' lives.

MONITORING NATURE RESERVES

Conservationists can fly drones over nature reserves to collect data on wildlife, their habitats and any threats that they face. This is often easier, cheaper, safer and more efficient than visiting these areas in person. It's particularly helpful for reserves in very dangerous or remote areas, as scientists don't have to risk becoming injured or stranded in the wild or getting caught up in local violence.

Quadcopter drones fly using four fast-spinning rotors. Moving similarly to helicopters, they can lift themselves straight into the sky and dart back and forth in different directions.

Fixed-wing drones look and move more like aeroplanes or gliders, with two wings and a central propeller. They are often built to fly over long distances and face harsh conditions.

LiDAR REMOTE SENSING

LiDAR (Light Detection and Ranging) is a way of building up a digital 3D picture of an area by shining lasers at a target surface. It works out distances by measuring the time it takes the light to leave the laser, to be reflected off a surface and to return to a sensor. Scientists can use LiDAR to study all sorts of natural habitats, from forests and cliff faces to the soil and the ocean floor.

LiDAR VISION

Some of the light in a laser beam will bounce off the first surface it hits (such as forest treetops), but the rest will pass through and only bounce back off a lower surface (such as the forest floor). Because LiDAR sensors can measure the intensity of the light at different points on its return journey, they can 'see' how it has travelled below the top surface.

An aircraft fitted with LiDAR sensors.

DID YOU KNOW?

Self-driving cars can use LiDAR to create 3D maps of areas as they're driving through them. Sensors look at the road ahead to check for conditions and obstacles.

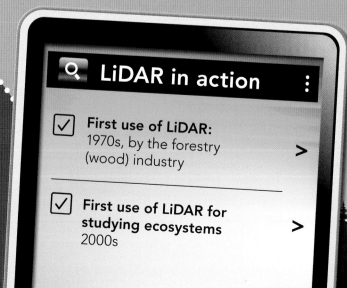

LiDAR in action

- ✓ **First use of LiDAR:** 1970s, by the forestry (wood) industry >

- ✓ **First use of LiDAR for studying ecosystems** 2000s >

POINT CLOUD MAPS

LiDAR data is used to create a 3D 'point cloud' map. This is a map made up of LiDAR measurement positions (points), and it can often contain millions of measurements. A 3D point cloud map can be zoomed in on and viewed from many different angles, so – for example – scientists can see individual trees' shapes and work out which tree species exist in that area.

HOW LiDAR CAN HELP US

LiDAR images offer a broad overview of an area but also provide a lot of detail, so they can give us a good idea of how healthy a habitat is and how conditions for wildlife are changing over time – often due to climate change or human activities.

This can help scientists to make plans for how best to work in the area. For example, they might suggest creating a nature reserve in a habitat with plenty of tree species that local wildlife rely on for food and shelter, rather than in a nearby area where many of these particular trees have died off or been cut down.

CITIZEN SCIENCE PROJECTS

Have you ever thought that you might like to become a scientist when you're older, helping to protect nature and wildlife yourself? Well, you don't need to wait – you can become a citizen scientist right now!

To take part in most citizen science projects, all you need is access to an internet-connected computer, tablet or smartphone.

HELPING THE PROFESSIONALS

Citizen science projects give volunteers the chance to get involved with scientific research, collecting and analysing data that helps professional scientists with their work. Many of these projects focus on nature and wildlife, with volunteers doing anything from counting butterflies in their local area to watching online videos from camera traps (see pages 6–7) and making a note of the different species of animals that appear.

Citizen scientists' efforts can help to cut down the manual work that scientists need to do, and give research projects much bigger data samples than could ever be collected and managed by staff alone. Their work can also help to test and improve computer programs and artificial intelligence systems, which scientists can use for their work in current and future projects.

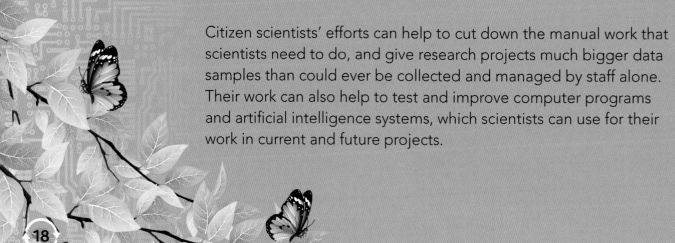

CITIZEN SCIENCE TECHNOLOGY

It might seem strange that you can do scientific research without specialised equipment, but we often take for granted just how advanced our everyday technology now is. An average smartphone today is far more powerful than the huge supercomputers that launched spacecraft to the Moon in the 1960s.

Citizen science projects typically have a website or app where you get instructions and submit your findings. Some projects are entirely online, while others ask you to explore your local area to collect data. The website or app has a hidden 'backend' area, with databases to store and sort this information so it's ready for scientists to examine. See page 31 for details of two popular citizen science websites.

See page 31 for details of two popular citizen science websites.

One citizen science project asks people to identify the age, sex and group size of beluga whales caught on underwater cameras. Expert-written instructions explain exactly what to look out for.

WILDLIFE SATELLITE TRACKING

Tracking wild animals helps us to better understand their movements, behaviours and the threats they face. Until around 65 years ago, researchers attached visible tags to animals but then had no way of following them – they just recaptured tagged animals when they spotted them. Since then, new tracking technologies have made things a bit easier.

FROM RADIO TO SATELLITE

First came radio tracking. Researchers fitted animals with transmitters that sent out radio waves, then followed the animal at close range by picking up the signal with an antenna and receiver.

Since 1978, we've tracked wildlife using satellites that circle around Earth and similarly use an antenna and receiver to pick up signals from animals' tags. Researchers don't need to stay close by; the satellite sends the information straight to their computer, wherever they are.

A satellite tracking tag is often visible, but can be inserted under an animal's skin to stop it getting in the way.

GLOBAL POSITIONING SYSTEM (GPS) TRACKING

GPS tracking, available since the 1990s (and used today for cars' sat-nav systems), involves animals wearing tags with receivers, rather than transmitters. The system uses data from one set of satellites to accurately track the animals' location and movement, then often uses another set of satellites to send this information to researchers' computers.

ROOM FOR IMPROVEMENT

Whether satellite tracking technology uses GPS or not, it still can't follow an animal absolutely everywhere on Earth. If animals are deep underwater or in a thick forest, the satellite can't communicate with their tags. Mammals that live in water are only 'visible' to the satellite when they come to the surface to breathe air.

DID YOU KNOW?

Satellite tracking tags can be powered by the Sun's energy. This makes them lighter than battery-powered versions, and avoids the problem of permanently losing contact with tags because their batteries have run out.

Since 2019, the International Space Station (ISS) has been used to track wildlife. It circles Earth more closely than most satellites, so it can pick up signals from tiny tags that weigh just 5 grams. These tags can be worn by small animals that couldn't previously be tracked.

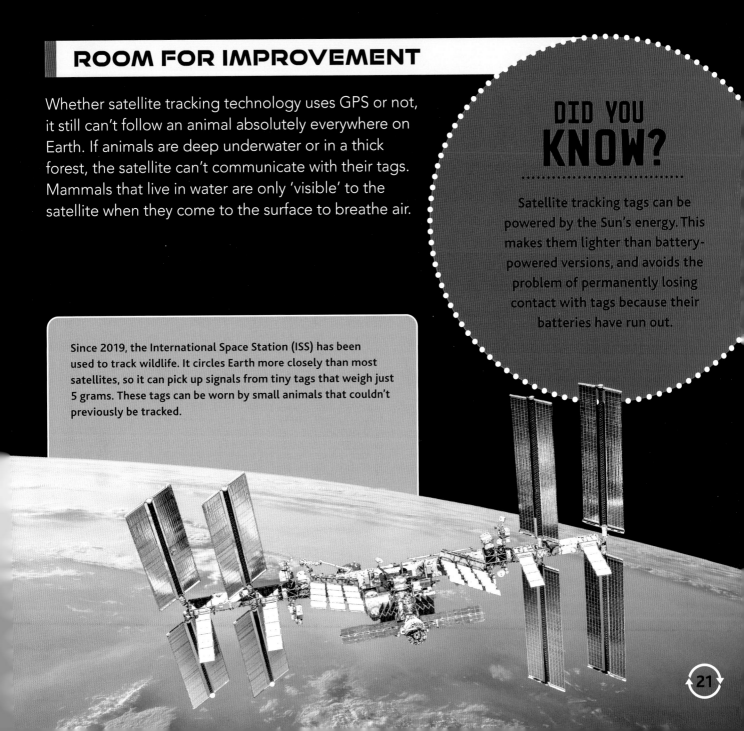

WILDLIFE CRIME DETECTION

The illegal wildlife trade is a huge global business worth around £17 billion a year. Criminals sell animals – often endangered species – for meat, ornaments and alternative medicines, or to keep as pets.

Some animals, such as elephants, rhinos, tigers, sea turtles, pangolins and seahorses, are particularly in demand and at greater risk of poaching.

Poachers usually carry guns or other weapons, putting nature reserve staff and other local people at serious risk. Nature reserve guards can sometimes respond by hurting or unfairly treating suspected poachers. This is obviously unacceptable – we need to use clever technology, rather than force, to stop wildlife crime.

Rhinos poached in South Africa, 2007–2019

2007:   13
2011:   448
2014:   1215
2019:   594

After a 9,000 per cent increase in rhino deaths from 2007 to 2014, conservation efforts – including the use of technologies – are having positive results.

DID YOU KNOW?

Scientists are trying to lower the value of rhino horn, making poaching much less worthwhile. They have created very convincing fake rhino horn made of horsehair and made it widely available to buy at a cheaper price.

Poacher-preventing technologies include camera traps, acoustic sensors (see pages 8–9), drones (see pages 14–15) and internet-connected sensors that alert nature reserve guards when they detect metal objects, such as cars, guns and knives.

But crime networks go far beyond poachers, who are often poor local people whom criminal gangs can easily replace. Technology can help us crack down on the transport and sale of illegal wildlife products, leading us closer to the big-time criminals running things – and stopping them making money.

Specially trained sniffer dogs can recognise traces of illegal wildlife objects in air samples from shipping containers, which officials collect using vacuum pumps.

✕ NO SALE

Lots of illegal wildlife trade now takes place online, often through social media. Researchers are developing artificial intelligence systems to help computers automatically identify and tag images and descriptions of illegal wildlife products. Suspicious posts could then be reported and removed, and the sellers potentially tracked down and arrested.

'GREEN' CITIES

All sorts of plants and animals live in cities, towns and suburbs rather than wild, remote areas – and they need our protection, too!

GREEN BUILDINGS

We can make space for nature in urban and suburban areas by covering buildings with plants to create roof gardens, green roofs and living walls. While birds and minibeasts enjoy the shelter and food sources, humans also benefit in many ways. The greenery can clean pollution from the air, improve people's mood and wellbeing, help to keep buildings warm in winter and cool in summer, and even give us fresh food to eat.

SAFE SPACES

We can help animals to roam safely in their habitat by creating wildlife crossings over roads and connecting up green urban areas with strips of undeveloped land. We can also make gardens and parks safer for wildlife by going low-tech, avoiding lawnmowers and weed-killing chemicals that can harm insects and other animals.

DID YOU KNOW?

More wild animals are moving into cities and suburbs because their natural habitats have been destroyed. There are now wild boar in Rome (Italy), leopards in Mumbai (India) and mountain lions in Los Angeles (USA).

DIM THE LIGHTS

Modern cities' dazzling electric lights can be confusing and harmful for wildlife. Some animals leave habitats if they're too bright, while others – such as moths – are so attracted by artificial light that it disrupts their feeding habits and stops them keeping themselves safe from predators and other dangers.

We can help by installing motion-detector lights, which only turn on (for a short time) when they sense nearby movement. We can also swap traditional lightbulbs for yellow-toned LED ones that are proven to attract fewer insects. Bonus: LEDs are also a greener, more energy-efficient option!

Some coastal cities have 'turtle-friendly' streetlights that give out a dim, red glow. This helps to stop newly hatched sea turtles getting confused by bright lights and heading towards nearby roads rather than into the ocean.

Cities gone wild

London – the world's first National Park City:

47 per cent green space, more than 8 million trees and around 13,000 animal species

Liberty Canyon, California, USA – the world's largest wildlife crossing:

Liberty Canyon Wildlife Crossing, due to open in 2023, will be a plant-covered bridge stretching 61 metres over a ten-lane motorway.

PHEROMONE TRAPS

Hungry animal pests can cause massive damage to farmers' crops. In poor, rural areas of the world, this can put farmers and other local people at great risk of starvation. Understandably, farmers often choose to use chemical pesticides to kill off these harmful insects and other animals.

Pests can harm important natural habitats as well as crops. These pheromone traps capture bark beetles to stop them destroying this pine forest.

However, chemical pesticides can also poison the soil, water and harmless local wildlife – including animal pollinators that help crops to grow. This can cause major long-term problems for farmers. Pheromone traps can help to control certain pests without seriously harming local ecosystems.

Pheromones

What are pheromones?
Natural chemicals that animals release to communicate with each other, often to attract mates for breeding. >

Pheromones first collected for research:
Late 1950s, from silkworm moths >

Number of insect species' pheromones now identified:
Around 1,500 >

DID YOU KNOW?

Climate change is creating warmer conditions that help many pests to breed in greater numbers. In 2019–20, Kenya had the worst invasion of locusts for 70 years – one swarm was around the size of 500 football pitches.

TRICKING INSECTS

Pheromone traps typically work by tricking males of a particular insect species into thinking they'll find females inside for mating. The traps contain artificial female pheromones, created by scientists in a laboratory.

First, scientists capture the smell of the female insect in an air sample. They use special machines – often ones called mass spectrometers – to work out which chemicals make up this smell. They then use another special machine, called an electroantennogram, to measure how the males' antennae respond to these chemicals.

The scientists mix together the chemicals that cause a reaction, and test this mixture on insects in the wild. Because the pheromones only attract males of a certain species, harmless local insects aren't affected.

THINKING AHEAD

Some pheromone traps have escape-proof designs, to capture lots of adult males so they're not available for mating. Others cover males in female pheromone powder to confuse and disrupt mating. Either way, the goal is the same: to limit breeding and therefore reduce the number of pests in the next generation.

Farmers and conservationists facing multiple pests have to put out different pheromone traps for each species.

INDIGENOUS LAND STEWARDING

Indigenous peoples are the descendants of those who lived in a country or area before others arrived and formed a new, dominant society. In their role as traditional guardians – or stewards – of their land, Indigenous peoples pass down knowledge through generations and maintain a deep, spiritual connection to nature and wildlife.

LISTEN AND LEARN

Indigenous peoples are some of the world's most effective conservationists. Their traditional knowledge respects the complexity of ecosystems and humans' responsibility to keep them healthy and balanced by living sustainably within them. Without this deep understanding of Earth's natural systems, flashy new conservation technologies can be ineffective or even cause unexpected problems.

DID YOU KNOW?

When Europeans settled in Australia around 230 years ago, the country's Indigenous peoples had already been living there for at least 65,000 years.

Indigenous Canadian chiefs and elders protest against plans to build a natural gas pipeline on their rightful land. Burning natural gas for fuel causes pollution and climate change, and drilling for it can pollute local water systems.

DRIVEN OUT

Indigenous peoples are often forced off their traditional lands by industries, such as mining and oil-drilling – and even by conservation projects. Instead of learning to better understand how Indigenous peoples can live amid nature without destroying it, those in charge of nature reserves and other protected areas often just drive out local communities – sometimes by using threats and serious violence.

TRADITIONAL TECHNOLOGIES

Technologies aren't just gadgets or computer-based systems – they're practical ways to use scientific knowledge. Indigenous eco-technologies include:

- growing food plants in the shade of trees rather than cutting down forests

- using natural materials to build homes, bridges and specialised structures, such as floating fish farms

- digging trenches and hidden wells to use water efficiently and cope during floods and droughts

- carefully planning out hunts – restricting them to limited numbers of animals at certain times of year, in particular areas – to get enough food without threatening any species' survival.

Indigenous Australian peoples traditionally use firesticks to burn off dry grass at certain times of year, to prevent serious fires caused by lightning strikes.

GLOSSARY

analyse to examine something in detail in order to explain it

antenna a device, often a long, thin metal rod, that sends or receives radio or TV signals

antennae long, thin body parts that certain animals use to smell and feel

atmosphere the layers of gases surrounding a planet or other object in space

climate change changes in long-term weather conditions and temperature patterns

conservationist someone who helps to protect nature and wildlife

data information, facts and figures collected and used to better understand something

deforestation cutting or burning down forest

ecosystem community of living things that interact with each other in an environment

endangered an endangered species is a type of living thing at risk of dying out

extinct describes a species that has completely died out and no longer exists

fossil fuel natural fuel, such as oil, that takes millions of years to form and can be burned for energy or heat

greenhouse gas gas that traps the Sun's heat in Earth's atmosphere, warming our planet

infrared energy waves that are often given out by warm objects but are invisible to humans

laser device that sends out a strong, thin, bright beam of light

microbes tiny living things that are too small to see unless you look through a microscope

mining digging valuable natural materials out of the ground

poaching killing or capturing animals illegally, often on someone else's land

satellite device sent into space to circle around Earth, collecting information or acting as part of a communication system

transmitter equipment that sends out messages via invisible radiation waves

trench long, narrow pit dug into the ground

vertebrate any animal, such as a mammal or fish, that has a backbone

well usually a deep hole dug in the ground to bring up water from below

FURTHER INFORMATION

If you're interested in getting involved in a Citizen Science project, ask a trusted adult to help you look for opportunities on websites such as scistarter.org and zooniverse.org. They should have a collection of projects that are suitable for children and young people.

BOOKS

Saving Species
by Jess French (Wren & Rook)

Meet amazing endangered animals from around the world and learn how conservationists are working to save them.

Caring for the Environment *(I'm a Global Citizen)*
by Georgia Amson-Bradshaw (Franklin Watts)

Find out how you can create positive, practical change and help to save our natural world.

The Incredible Ecosystems of Planet Earth
by Rachel Ignotofsky (Wren & Rook)

Discover how Earth's huge variety of ecosystems work, from deserts and rainforests to a single drop of water.

VIDEOS

How community-led conservation can save wildlife:
youtube.com/watch?v=pR83Woy0zDs

Lion conservationist Dr Moreangels Mbizah explains why it's so important that people know and care about the animals living in their local area.

Endangered Species: Worth Saving from Extinction?
youtube.com/watch?v=h5eTqjzQZDY

Why exactly do we try to protect endangered species from dying out? Find out in this video!

INDEX